THE MOUNTAINS THAT MADE ME

Articulations of Poetry
by

SIERRA DEAN

Copyright © 2016 by Sierra Dean

All Rights Reserved. No part of this publication may be reproduced in any form or by any means including, scanning, photocopying, or otherwise without prior written permission from the author.

ISBN:978-0-9975042-0-0

Edited by Flora Brown

Cover Design by Max Photo Master

Headshot Image by Tonya Shotz

Printed in the United States of America

To order additional copies of this book, contact the author:

Sierra Dean
sierra.dean@deandiaries.com
www.deandiaries.com

DEDICATION

Sylvia Brown was my mother's very close friend. She was more like an aunt that I never had. She was an amazing woman that was always ready to let go of her hurt and pain. She knew that she could always do better and was never afraid. I only remember wonderful and really funny memories of Sylvia. Even though she showed everyone else that she was strong, she was living another life at home in fear. She was a domestic violence victim that was killed by her partner after she was ready to leave him. Her situation really helped me to realize that all women have a story and we need to share them with each other to keep us strong.

I love you Sylvia, this is for you.

TABLE OF CONTENTS

DEDICATION iii
INTRODUCTION: THIS SOFT SPOKEN
GIRL HAS PROBLEMS TOO 1
I CAN'T WAIT 5
I THOUGHT I WAS HAPPY 7
WHERE MY TESTIMONY BEGINS 9
I WANT THAT FEELING 19
BEING SELFISH TO MYSELF 21
LET GO 23
EVERYTIME 25
LOVE 27
MISSING YOU 29
THIS THING CALLED DATING 33
TOO MUCH FOR YOU 35
COMPLETE ME 37
FRIENDSHIP ENDS 39
ME 41
WHAT DO YOU SEE? 43
WHERE DO WE STAND? 45
I'M SORRY 47

ALL I ASK 49
WHERE YOU WANT TO BE 51
THE CRAVE 53
A MAN? REALLY 55
SO OVER YOU 57
FRIENDS TO ENEMIES 59
SINGLE OR NO? 61
I WISH I HAD A SAY SO 63
TAKE ME FROM THIS COLD PLACE 67
CRYING IN SILENCE 71
WHAT I DON'T HAVE 73
WHY DON'T YOU WANT ME 75
FORCING SOMETHING NOT THERE 77
BEING HAPPY WITH YOURSELF 79
WHERE DID YOU GO 81
BEFORE THE INTERVIEW 83
AFTER THE INTERVIEW 85
FINALLY REALIZED WHY I MET YOU 87
I'M SMILING NOW 89
IT'S TIME FOR YOU TO GET OVER
YOUR MOUNTAINS 91
ABOUT THE AUTHOR 119

INTRODUCTION: THIS SOFT SPOKEN GIRL HAS PROBLEMS TOO

There was a point in my life when I didn't know what to do with my problems. I felt like everyone was living their dreams and just happy as they could be, while I was sick to my stomach because my problems were becoming too overwhelming for me to cope with. Nobody else knew my struggles or what I was going through; well at least that's what I thought. My hurt and pain was beginning to take over my way of thinking and I wasn't sure what to do about it.

Then there was that moment when I picked up an empty notebook and began writing down my true feelings. The first day, I really enjoyed my journaling so much that I just stayed in the house writing all day long. At that point, I realized that I was having a conversation with myself and started to gain clarity about my feelings. Nobody was there to judge me and nobody was there to give me their opinions, which was wonderful. It was just me, my paper and my pen.

As you read this book, you will notice that I have included questions for you to think about throughout the poems. Those are some of the questions that went through my head as I was going through my situations.

There's a journaling section in the back of the book for you to answer those questions. I'm sure that you will find yourself questioning what I did or maybe you were in the same situation. I want you to take the time to write down your true feelings because believe me; journaling will get you through your situations.

It's nothing like your own story.

"Sometimes the strongest among us are the ones who smile through silent pain, cry behind closed doors and fight battles nobody knows about."

~Unknown~

I CAN'T WAIT

I can't wait until the day I can wake up, be happy and content with my life.

I can't wait until the day I know that someone will be waiting on me to come home.

I can't wait until the day that I can wake up with all of my bills paid.

I can't wait until the day when I am financially stable.

I can't wait until the day I get another promotion.

I can't wait until the day I can walk down the aisle giving my life to someone else who I know will love and take care of me.

I can't wait until the day I come home and the love of my life has dinner, flowers, and a massage waiting.

I can't wait until the day I can have a child and become a mom.

I can't wait until the day....

I THOUGHT I WAS HAPPY

Sometimes I ask myself

Am I happy?

Am I at the place that I want to be right now?

Could things be better or will I even allow things to be better?

It seems like everything that I used to have is fading away slowly

Is it my fault because I didn't make wise decisions?

Why blame anyone else when this is my life that I'm living?

Once everyone is gone, will I still be here battling with myself?

Someone recently told me that I don't seem as happy as I used to be

Am I letting my problems and issues take over my life?

Did I just forget how to cope with everything?

Is it that I just don't have the right person in my life to help me keep my head above water when I'm drowning?

I can only motivate myself so much just so that I will make it through

At times I get so frustrated and tired that I just don't know what to do

Lord in the name of Jesus I do thank you for bringing someone into my life to guide me along the way at a very young age

I know that it was a blessing and a trial

I thank you for putting me through that

At the time I was wondering why me

Why was I going through this?

Will I ever get out?

But it only made me stronger

I ask myself again

Am I happy?

Why should I have to ask myself this question when I should already know...?

WHERE MY TESTIMONY BEGINS

Why would you lie to me?

How could you not tell me the truth?

Were you puzzled on what to say because we just had a conversation about this the other day?

Maybe that was your opportunity to be real

Maybe you were just too afraid of how I would feel

You decided to be with me and I was just content being friends

You kept telling me that you didn't want this to end

From partying all night to staying up late

Having so much fun

We rarely went on dates

All I wanted was time and that's what I got

You gave me so much love;

The love that I thought I was able to take

Then there came the times when I was bailing

you out of jail left and right

To me arguing with your baby moma about to fight

I'm not the kind of person that likes drama

I never really wanted to be with anybody with a baby moma

You were always out in the streets on the block

In my kitchen making rocks

Always saying that you would be on top

On top of your shit

On top with another hustle

All I really saw was a struggle

I never understood why I wanted to stay

Come to think of it

You always had the right words to say

From I love you

To baby I will never leave you

To baby just trust me

And I did

That one night while sitting on the bed

I will never forget the conversation

I wanted to pour my heart out to you because I was feeling so much frustration

You laid there listening to me as if you cared

Now I look back

All I could see is your eyes in a blank stare

I sat there and cried as I told you that I wanted a child

A child of my own and a huge home

I told you I had an abortion when I was 16

How much I grieved

I had several miscarriages

That I knew I was able to conceive

You told me

Baby it's not your time as you can see

I said maybe that is true but I want to carry your

baby and be your wife to be

I sat there crying my heart out until I went to sleep

Not knowing if you even heard a peep

Of what I actually said, because you just laid there in the bed

Time went on as if this conversation never happened

Maybe that was just something I imagined

We were together for about 6 months after you ended your relationship with the last girlfriend you stayed with

A difference happened overtime and I believe that was when you found out

The beginning of something that would change my life once I found out about

Saturday morning walking my dog in the park as I would normally do

Then I called you to see what you were up to

You were drunk at 1 o'clock as I looked at the time on my phone

Then I said bye and there was a dial tone

Something wasn't right this day and I knew it wasn't

But then I said to myself stop tripping, you're always fussing

Went scrolling through Facebook while I sat on my friend's bed

And then I saw something that made me feel as if I was hit in the head

You were holding baby clothes with your ex-girlfriend at a baby shower standing next to a baby bed

Is this true?

This can't be

Let me just call him so that I can see

Then all I could do was curse because my heart was broken into pieces

I poured my heart out to you and all I got was grievance

Drinking bottle after bottle until I couldn't anymore

I just want to go to sleep because the inside of my body felt so sore

Nobody knew my pain

I told my friends and family because I needed someone to talk to

But nobody understood all of the pain I was going through

The next day all I could do was lay there

I thought it was all a dream

But this was very real

The pain I felt seemed like it would never heal

I felt so alone

So empty inside

All I wanted to do was hide

Hide away from the world

Hide away from the pain

Because I felt as if I had nothing to gain

I had nothing to offer a man

I couldn't carry a child

I felt this pain for so many hours

I laid on the couch drinking my life away

Nobody called because I guess they didn't know what to say

Nothing was making me feel better

Not even the liquor

I thought that I might as well do something bigger

I went to the medicine cabinet

Gathered everything that I could

Started taking whatever because if the pain was gone I will feel good

Better than what I was going through

I just couldn't take it

Then I passed out on the couch lying on my stomach

My heartbeat was so loud

All I heard was it pounding

I never heard my heartbeat so loud but I didn't care

I just wanted it to be over

At that moment, I felt that it was over

Was I being selfish?

Was I just giving up?

I was thinking so many things

I didn't care because the pain made me feel like my heart was shrinking

I believe that I stopped breathing because my body was so cold

All I could think was that the pain is over now

However, I guess that's not how it goes....

I opened my eyes wondering what happened

Why was I still here?

This was not how I imagined

I got up crying in a deep puddle of tears

Then got my journal and started to write down

all of my fears

It was not my time and it was not time for me to go

I knew that because over time, my life started telling me so

Now four years later, I'm so grateful that it was not me being his baby moma or wife to be

Looking on Facebook, I see him teaching his son how to shoot dice

Smoking weed and flashing money

That's not how I want my life to be

I'm just glad that it's not me

Now I'm helping women to get themselves out of horrible situations because I know that they were once me

Nobody deserves to go through any heartache and pain

Now that I don't want to see

I don't want to see another woman lying on the couch like me.

During this time, lying on my couch knowing

that I just attempted suicide, I felt as if nobody loved me and nobody would care if I was gone. I realize now that I was being selfish and only thinking of myself. After feeling like my life was gone, I still felt hurt and pain. I was confused trying to figure out why I was still feeling this way. I believe that I had a conversation with the All Mighty God while I was gone and it wasn't my time. He kept me.

Have you ever felt like giving up on everything?

I WANT THAT FEELING

I really want a child, baby, kid or whatever your choice of name

Why was I never blessed with that feeling?

Did I not do the right thing?

Maybe I didn't

Was I not with the right person?

Maybe I wasn't

Will I ever have that sensation of feeling a baby kick inside of me?

Will I ever be able to have that morning sickness to let me know that I'm pregnant?

Will I ever be able to make it past four months and be able to buy maternity clothes?

Why was I never blessed with this feeling?

It makes me so sad some days, but I still smile as if everything is okay.

I want that feeling of knowing that someone needs me to survive

Why do I feel as if I'm surviving for no reason because I have no one to depend on me?

I guess I will never have this feeling

I can't feel this for the rest of my life

I ask myself, should I adopt or get an implant?

But I want the real thing

It seems as if the real thing will never happen

I feel so sad over this situation

Please let me know how I am supposed to cope.

Some people don't understand how having a child is such a huge blessing. I've always wanted a child to call my own but I know that one day my time will come.

If you've ever felt this way or know someone that is having a hard time having children, don't brush this under a rug. There's a much bigger situation going on deep inside.

BEING SELFISH TO MYSELF

I was in love once upon a time

Was so hurt it almost felt like a crime

Some folks say I was blind

Maybe it just wasn't at the right time

It seems like the time I spent came back to haunt me

Why does it have to be this way?

With this heart so cold

It seems like it was never made of gold

I know that I can shine like the light

Butitseemslikeit'salwaysafight

Maybe I'm afraid

Afraid to be me;

But what can I say

It's time to see.

Have you ever been in love with someone but it seemed like you weren't your complete self around them; you only hang on so that you wouldn't lose them?

How did that make you feel? Maybe you just did it because it was completing your happiness at the moment or maybe it was just the thrill of living a lie.

Just take a moment to write down why your complete self was not your complete self at that moment.

LET GO

There is something inside of me that won't let go of you

Something inside of me that just wants to keep a hold on you

I can't determine what you did to me to make me feel this way

I don't want to actually be with you but I can't let you go

How you make me feel is indescribable

It's unimaginable

How can I determine what you did to me?

Maybe there is no explanation

You are such a wonderful person and need to find someone true

Someone who will truly be there for you

How can you find that person if I keep holding on to you?

I push you away and you come right back

Maybe   it's   fate?

But I really don't think that's the case

I just need to go ahead and give you your space because it's time for me to be replaced.

EVERYTIME

Every time I think of you

I think of that soft touch

That moment when everything seems to be gone

How is it that you make me feel as if this is not real?

Maybe it's just too good to be true as Lauren Hill would say "I can't keep my eyes off you"

You make me feel good in every way

There are so many things I could say

Do I really want you to know that I feel this way?

Why can't you see?

Maybe you're blind or just stunting because I'm on your mind?

I'm sure this is not what you want

This was not in the plan but I just wonder if you ever thought of being my man?

Every time I think of you a sensation flows through me

Maybe it's just going too deep?

I really can't figure out where this is all coming from

I just feel like sometimes I need to run

Away from my feelings

Away from my future

Away from you because I'm sure this won't last

Why should I feel this way to just runaway?

Maybe it's me

There's still more I could say

Every time I think of you

I want you more

I just love it

It just feels so good from your every touch

Maybe I should flee

I think of you too much.

LOVE

Why does love make me feel this way?

Leaves me speechless with no words to say

I can't believe you hurt me like this

But then you want to turn around and give me a kiss

Love is supposed to be patient and kind

Where was mine?

I have yet to find

Someone that is true

Someone who is you

Maybe it will come one day

Just not today

Love makes me feel wonderful then hurts me to where I can't take it

Love hurts in more ways than one

Physically, emotionally, and financially

I just can't take it anymore

Is this what love is about?

Maybe it's just lust?

There's always so much fuss around the word love

Are you forcing this love?

It's not real

Seems so hard to find

I assume one day

I will find mine.

MISSING YOU

So I'm feeling this way

I don't even want to say

That I'm missing you

Why did you make me feel this way?

You used to comfort me at night

That I can no longer find

You gave me peace of mind

Even though the love was blind

I gazed into your eyes

All I see is me

But why am I feeling this way, when I know it's not meant to be?

You hurt me so bad that I can't even say

You make me feel as if I want you to stay

Now when I see you I get angry

When you leave I feel so hungry

Hungry for that love

That life

That wonderful peace of mind

I'm speaking on it because the love is still blind

You make me feel free,

With nowhere else to be

Why do I miss you?

When it was so hard to see that the love was blind

Now I'm where I wanted to be

No one can make me feel the way that you did and the feeling was real

I can only say how I feel

I still love you but I know it could never be

I'm at the place now where I need to be.

Have you ever been so in love with someone that it made you blind to reality? You know that you are not meant to be with this person but you still hope that one day they will change. Then, you realize they will change when it's too late?

THIS THING CALLED DATING

So you say that you want to be with me

You don't even know me

You have no idea how I roll or who I hang with

How can I just be with you?

Do you just want sex because that's just not something I do?

You want me to be your boo

You have no clue what I do and what I'm into

Do you have a good head on your shoulders?

I bet you think I do

Yet you still want me to be your boo

How could you fall so easily?

Is this a trap or a setup?

Now I don't trust you

You want me to be your boo

What are you really into?

What do you really want to do?

I don't think you have a clue.

TOO MUCH FOR YOU

Can anyone really handle me?

How out of control I can be

You can't really tame me

You can train me

To be the woman you want me to be

Deep down inside, there still lies that uncontrollable me

That one that doesn't listen

That one that is stubborn

That one that has a short fuse

That one that loves to hide

Hide behind the pain and behind the love

Can anyone really handle me?

I don't think they can

Something may be wrong with you

Maybe could be just being a man.

Step up to the plate and hold me down

Keep me on track

If you don't, it may be a wrap

So sorry to tell you I'm out of control;

Pretty face pretty smile

The thirst still grows

Wants to be wild

Wants to run free

Can anyone really handle me?

I guess we shall see.

COMPLETE ME

Nobody will never understand my pain at night

The cries in my head when I can't sleep

The nights when I toss and turn

Look over with nobody to turn to

Everyone sees a wonderful person on the outside

They don't see the pain growing inside

How do I manage to feel this way?

Sometimes it's so hard to speak

I don't know where my brain will be.

The hazard lights are on and I'm losing control

Of what was and what is,

Tell me, where is my soul?

I want to be true

I want to be complete

I just can't take the anxiety

I need to fill something that needs to be complete

Tell me what it could be

What can't I see?

FRIENDSHIP ENDS

Well I guess it's the end

The end of our friendship

That never really began

We knew each other as sisters

How could you hurt me?

You know my heart is sensitive

But now we have to flee

Away from our love Away from our

friend

Away from the kind hearts, that used to be

We knew each other for years

Now it seems as if we knew each other for weeks

Now my heart feels cold

As cold as it can be

Why do we need to leave each other?

I really don't want to feel this

way

I just can't find the words to say that

I really want you to stay

In my life forever

Will it ever be the same?

Now I don't even want to say your name

ME

I am a free spirit

I am able to open my arms to others open heartedly

I live everyday gracefully and thankful for everything I have

I love my life but I can always make it better

I just choose to be me

I live through me and not through others as you plainly see

I have my own style and my own path

I choose to be free

Not a follower

Only a leader

Never wanting to be like the next person

There is only one me

WHAT DO YOU SEE?

So you stare at me as I walk pass switching my hips and licking my lips

Do you really want me?

Do you just want what you see?

Would you want me once you get to know me?

Would you leave once you realize the person that I grew up to be?

I wake up every morning with my weave down my back

Make up my face just to get my life back on track

I refuse to leave the house without completing one or the other

I'm afraid of what people will discover

The real me

The person I grew up to be

Would you still want me once my weave is gone and my face is uncovered?

This doesn't last long once we get under the cover rolling around with each other

You will really discover the real me

The person I grew up to be

How can I become one with you if I can't face the fact that real beauty is true?

I will just keep walking, switching my hips and licking my lips

Wondering about my next beauty tip

Now do you still want me or do you just like what you see?

Until you discover the person I grew up to be

I'm happy with the person I look in the mirror and see

Or, am I just looking at me materialistically?

WHERE DO WE STAND?

While I sit here and gather my thoughts

Why do you keep running through my head?

I'm trying to understand every word that was said

I don't know where this is going

Where is it coming from?

I must ask

What has been in your head?

Do you want to stop?

Put this to an end

Or, do you just want me to be your friend?

I really don't want to take this any further than it already is.

But I just can't seem to figure out what you did

Maybe it was what you said

I just need to back away before I get sad

I'm very emotional and I don't want you to experience

The pain I go through when things start to get serious

So at this time it needs to be over

I'M SORRY

I'm sorry that I made you feel this way

I'm sorry that I hurt you

Will you ever accept my apologies or is this something that you cannot do?

Why don't I care, but then I really do? You're too sensitive

Or I just love being an asshole to you

Would you think I'm really sincere?

Should I just go away with no fear?

No fear of where this will go or where it will end

I know that we do need to put this to amends

Just let go,

Then I ask, is my apology really sincere?

I can hear myself speaking, but it's still unclear.

ALL I ASK

I have this strong stimulation flowing through my bones

There is one thing that I want you to do

I want you to make me feel wonderful so that I can just fiend for you

I want you to mold my body to yours

That's just something that I would really adore I

want you to make me feel a special type of way,

I want you to bring me fire, passion and desire

Only until I'm tired

Once it starts again let's bring something new

I want you to give me you and all of you,

That's all I want you to do

Now is that too much to ask?

I'm sure you're thinking

That's true.

WHERE YOU WANT TO BE

Relationships, but then you don't want to be in one

Now you wonder why I say I'm done

Want to go on dates

Then you leave and just say I'm sorry boo

Back to the streets

I need time for me too

How could that be?

You want me to be loyal

Then don't answer my call

I'm wondering what if I ever fall

Need your help

Where would you be?

In the streets?

Talking about you need to be free

You don't want a relationship

So treat it as so

Then you and I can move on

Now you're free to go.

THE CRAVE

Temptation...Temptation comes in many different forms

You crave it

You want it

You know you shouldn't have it

It's something that you want to stay

It's not good for you

You still want it more and more

What will you get from it?

Satisfaction that lasts only a moment

Then it's just an instant

Instant need for satisfaction

Maybe you need to do something else to let go of that crave

It's one thing that just doesn't go away in days

You try to get rid of it but it keeps coming back

Like a letch that keeps getting attached

It's a feeling of want and need

We all know that those are two separate things Temptation will last for a lifetime if you let it

You know it's not healthy

Someday the temptation will stop

When will that be?

Only time will tell

Until then I will still hold on to that letch.

A MAN? REALLY

So you think you're a man?

Running around in the streets but can't find a place to eat or sleep

Thinking you're taking care of your kids

Just to take them back home to the baby moma

Teaching them how to curse and sag

Which calls for drama

Now you wonder why your child is going to school cursing and getting put out

Remember you taught her that this was cool

Then you ask her... why do you want to act like a fool? Remember daddy you taught her this

Just the other day she learned to French kiss

So now, you think you're a man?

Wondering what's going on with your boys?

Why they want to play with girls instead of toys

Remember daddy you taught him this

Now you have to figure out what you missed

Too busy running in the streets

Then wonder why you can't get any peace

No place to sleep

Now you got beef

Beef with the baby moma

How hard could this be?

Running back and forth to your kid's school Remember you told them this was cool

Now you realize this is not a game

It's part of life

For some reason you can't seem to explain

So you think you're a man?

How about you think again?

Don't think too hard because you might go insane.

SO OVER YOU

Now you want to try to come back in my life

You know before you left I put up a mighty fight

A fight within myself and a fight with you

Now you want to come talking about "I miss you"

Well this time I moved on and I hope you do the same

This time there is only one person to blame

You said you didn't want this and you weren't ready

Now you on the phone with me sounding real petty

Asking who I'm with and where I'm going

Can you just go somewhere?

Go get a job and get off my line

You're not even worth a dime

Actually not even worth my time

I can't believe I put up with so much

I never want you back is all I can say now

You only miss what you had when it's gone

It's only so much that I can allow

I'm so over this and I'm so over you

Just get off my line because you're way overdue.

FRIENDS TO ENEMIES

Here we go again back down this road

From friends to lovers to enemies

When will this ever end?

I used to love you as a friend

Then one day I thought you would be my man

Then you started acting crazy

Now you're back to my enemy again

How and why is this happening?

You get mad because I'm not giving you what you want

How could I when you're crazy and act like a cunt?

I guess we will someday go back to being friends

Then to enemies again

You need to understand

With you being my man

That has to come to an end

*You messed up a long time
ago*

*I wish we could start all the way back where we
began.*

SINGLE OR NO?

Do I want to be single or in a relationship?

I keep asking my friends for tips

One will say "It's okay I love the single life"

Another will say "I can't seem to find one my type"

But then I always think about someone holding me at night

I realize this is not right

I can't be single because I feel alone

Then I feel like I'm all wrong

Being in a relationship is hard with a lot of commitment

I'm not really ready for that because people put me through so much shit

I can't even express the way I feel to people anymore

I only accept their feelings but then they look at me wanting more

Should I remain single to figure out where I want to be?

I want that relationship feeling just so that you

can hold me

Comfort me

Make me feel wanted

Hold me so tightly

Then I will tell you that you drive me crazy

I'm so confused on if I should be single or not;

Then I just think I'm not going to put my feelings on the spot

Let you go

Maybe so

I WISH I HAD A SAY SO

So as I walk up to this building to everyone holding a sign

I'm thinking this is a horrible idea

I wish this time I was blind

Blind to the true fact that I was about to let this happen

Blind to the angry faces

I do not want to know who is watching

Watching me walk into this building to do something horrible

It wasn't really my fault

It's just that I got caught

Caught in this web I can't seem to get out of

I really don't want to do this, but I'm young and don't know any better

Filling out these papers and still wondering why

Looking at the confusion, anger, frustration, and guilt on everyone's face

*There is only so much of this that I can
take*

*Please call me so that I can get this over
with*

*I really don't want to do this, but I'm still young
and my say so doesn't count*

*Now I'm walking down these stairs and into a
room*

No one says anything

I'm thinking that I just want out

*Out of this place that I don't want
to be*

*Please I wish I was blind right now because I
can't stand what I see*

*A white room with doctors all
around me*

A bucket at the end of this table

About to catch what is inside of me

Please get this over with

*Now all I can hear is a
plop*

I can't believe I did this

I'm in shock

Now I'm home sick as hell wondering what I just did

Laying on this bed of mine

Knowing that I just got rid of my kid.

Did you know someone who had an abortion? Have you ever had an abortion? Maybe you can't stand the thought of abortion. How does this subject truly make you feel?

TAKE ME FROM THIS COLD PLACE

I can hear my heart beat

As my body gets cold

Then I can barely see

My eyes closed

Looking at what I've done

How did it come to this?

Everyone's life is a trip

But why did I think mine would be different?

Maybe if I pray I would wake back up

Maybe if I sleep I would feel no suffer

Pain or powerless

The struggle within deepens

I wonder where I am

Am I here?

Am I in another place?

I don't want a second chance

I just want the pain to end

Why did I end up this way?

With this same feeling all day

I know that nothing will change

I just can't seem to put my mind away from the pain

I know I was gone

I heard my heart beating in my head

It was loud

The pain in my heart

I could still feel the suffer

My body was numb

I could feel nothing

My mind still wondered in circles

I guess this is what happens when your soul is dead

CRYING IN SILENCE

Nobody will ever know the pain I feel inside

When my heart begins to hurt

I lay down and cry

Cry for so many reasons

This seems to be too much to me

With no one to call when my body is suffering

Feeling pain from my past, present and future

No one will ever know how I really feel inside

They may call me crazy

So I just run and hide away from it all

Then the tears just flow

I know why I'm crying but no one will ever know.

WHAT I DON'T HAVE

I understand that I am not a perfect individual

Why is it that I turn my head at other people having children or starting a family?

What's wrong with me?

What did I miss?

Why is it so hard for me to find a person just to kiss?

One good time on the lips is all I need

I want to have that wonderful feeling inside that I greed

Some say you don't need that because you are free to do what you want to do

I guess they don't know me

I know myself and its plain to see I'm not happy with only just me

I want to have someone say he loves me every day and he misses me

I want to come home to kids yelling "Mommy"

This will make me feel free

Right now I'm living this life that I enjoy only to a degree

I just want that time where I can be my kind of free.

WHY DON'T YOU WANT ME?

How can I express in words how I really feel about you?

How you make my heart race every time I see your face

How I wish I always was the one with you on a date

How can I say this without being hurt?

Well it can always turn out worse

Why is it that I feel you love me but some days you really don't?

Why won't you be honest with me, am I really the one you want?

Let me know and I won't complain

Maybe it's for the best

I will let you explain the rest.

I remember being in love with someone that was not in love with me. That feeling was great when he was around, but once he was gone, I knew that he was with someone else. I always tried to convince myself otherwise, but now I realize that I deserved so much more.

FORCING SOMETHING NOT THERE

What are you to do when the person that you love doesn't want the same lifestyle as you?

Do you leave them or just deal with it until they begin to feel the way you do?

Why is it that you can wake up with someone not knowing what will happen next?

Aren't you supposed to wake up looking at the person and say "I'm so lucky to have you in my life and you complete me"?

Why do we let ourselves fall short from what we really want?

Is it that we put others before ourselves in order to make someone else's life happy?

How can we say that we are in love when we are not really on that same page?

Are we still chasing the past hoping that it will lead us to the future?

What are you really in love with?

The person?

Intimacy?

Or just the fact that you are with someone?

How can you be happy with someone if they are not on the same page as you?

BEING HAPPY WITH YOURSELF

Why is it that the happiest people are really the saddest?

Is it their way of hiding all of the hurt that they are going through or went through?

It's like as long as others around them are happy and smiling it makes everything better

I wonder why it's so hard to say how you feel, but I guess it's nobody's business but your own

It's like if you walk around sad, everyone will ask you what's wrong left and right

Nobody wants that

It's just crazy that in order to keep composure, someone has to be happy around them

Did people forget how to make themselves happy and feel good?

Maybe everyone should make a list of what he or she enjoy doing without the presence of others.

My thing is, how will you ever be happy when the only way that you know how is through others?

People will not always be there when you need them

So find what makes you happy without the presence of others.

Have you ever had that moment where you felt alone? All you wanted to do was be around a group of people just to have so much fun for a moment but when you came back home, you realized that reality never went anywhere?

How did you feel when you were in that moment?

WHERE DID YOU GO

I feel as if I'm losing everything slowly

I get so afraid that I may lose it

Will they only look at the bad and not at the good?

I used to have someone to talk to

Someone that would listen and give me advice

Now I just have someone that only listens

You never really realize what you have until it's gone

I want that feeling back

Will I ever have someone in my life again that I would be able to talk to?

I really don't ask for much

Only for love, attention, communication and just be there for me.

Was there ever a point in your life where you felt alone? Maybe you had a close friend that is no longer in your life to talk to and now you can't find anyone you can trust.

How does that make you feel and why can't you talk to anyone?

WHERE DID YOU GO

I feel as if I'm losing everything slowly

I get so afraid that I may lose it

Will they only look at the bad and not at the good?

I used to have someone to talk to

Someone that would listen and give me advice

Now I just have someone that only listens

You never really realize what you have until it's gone

I want that feeling back

Will I ever have someone in my life again that I would be able to talk to?

I really don't ask for much

Only for love, attention, communication and just be there for me.

Was there ever a point in your life where you felt alone? Maybe you had a close friend that is no longer in your life to talk to and now you can't find anyone you can trust.

How does that make you feel and why can't you talk to anyone?

BEFORE THE INTERVIEW

While I sit here waiting patiently

I'm getting more nervous as the minutes go by

What will they think of me when they first see my face?

How will they fill about the words I'm going to say?

There is only one outcome

Either a yes or no

There is never a maybe so

Or maybe next time

I really want a yes but in the end I will still know that I am blessed

Blessed to have this experience

To find my new journey

I know that I'm ready for this, but will they really understand?

Understand that I'm passionate

In what I'm trying to say

Well here they are

Now here I go.

AFTER THE INTERVIEW

Well now that it's over and I'm not really sure what to think

Did they want to consider me as a candidate?

Or did I talk too much again?

I think I did because I really want this role

I know that I can do well and be all I can be and more,

I wish that I was able to find out the outcome today

I'm sure that won't happen

I'm wondering what it will be

I'm honestly so tired of filling out these applications

For some reason I'm starting not to believe in me

But everyone else does

My confidence is growing thin

I'm not sure how this will end

I hope that I don't give up and keep going

Then I still have to wait but I don't have patience

I'm sure it will be another "no" like always because there's someone else that is much better than me

We shall see how this goes

Let's see if I will finally get my chance to grow.

Being on this interview made me notice that my hurt was affecting my way of thinking. I was starting to doubt myself so much in many situations. My friends and family were the ones who were able to encourage me to believe in myself.

Are there times where you doubted yourself too much?

FINALLY REALIZED WHY I MET YOU

God will bring people in your life for a reason

It's always a time and a season for everything and everyone

Just never try to take advantage when you're given one

There's always a need for something in your life and you can't get there without another person

Once this has been realized, everything will be a lot easier to deal with

You will learn how to understand and love everyone for who they are

Don't get me wrong; some people come into your life and bring you down

But there's always someone there to jump in and pick you right back up

Nothing will always be perfect in life

Know that not everyone is brought into your life for a lifetime

It's only a season and a reason

Keep loving yourself and your neighbor

Most importantly love the All Mighty because he is the one making all of this happen

No one can get to a great place in life without going through the bad

Everyone is brought into your life for a reason and a season

I'M SMILING NOW

I am smiling because by the grace of God I made it through

I am smiling because I could have been dead but he called someone to help me

I am smiling because I could be without a car but by the grace of God he provided me with a job

I am smiling because by the grace of God he woke me up this morning

I am smiling because by the grace of God he started me on my way to where I was headed today

I am smiling because he brought someone in my life of whom I can talk to about my problems

I am smiling because he watched over me while I was sleeping last night

I am smiling because he helped me to pay my bills last week

I am smiling because I am content with my situation right now

I am smiling because I am able to know why I am smiling.

I am smiling because I'm able to write this down

I am smiling because he has forgiven me of my sins

I am smiling because many love me

I am smiling because I'm blessed

I am smiling because this is not the end.

IT'S TIME FOR YOU TO GET OVER YOUR MOUNTAINS

Now that you've read my story, it's time to write yours. There is a reason that you have this book. The Mountains That Made Me is not just a title, but there is true meaning behind these five words. I went through some rough Mountains and struggled so much along the way. It took so much courage to write this book but I was able to make it out. I was able to survive to tell my story because I know that there is another Sierra Dean out there.

I want you to take some time to write down how you truly feel. I know you will definitely start to get over your Mountains also.

Be careful how you are talking to yourself because you are listening.
~Lisa. M. Hayes~

I didn't always know what I wanted to do, but I knew the kind of woman I wanted to be.
~Diane Von Furstenberg~

Believe in yourself and all that you are. Know that there is something inside of you that is greater than any obstacle.
~Christian D. Larson~

Nothing makes a woman more Beautiful than the belief that she is Beautiful.

~Sophia Loren~

As you become more clear about who you really are, you'll be better able to decide what is best for you the first time around.

~Oprah Winfrey~

You will face many defeats in your life, but never let yourself be defeated.
~Maya Angelou~

Never apologize for being sensitive or emotional. Let this be a sign that you've got a big heart and aren't afraid to let others see it. Showing your emotions is a sign of strength.
~**Brigitte Nicole**~

In the end, some of your greatest pain become your greatest strength.
~Unknown~

Sometimes you have to go through things and not around them.

~Unknown~

It's better to be alone rather than being with someone who makes you feel like you're alone.

~Unknown~

> *We must be willing to let go of the life we have planned,*
> *so as to have the life that is waiting for us.*
> ~E.M. Forster~

Nothing can bring you peace but yourself.
~Ralph Waldo Emmerson~

If we wait until we're ready, we'll be waiting for the rest of our lives.
~**Lemony Snicket**~

A strong, positive, self-image is the best possible preparation for success in life.
~Dr. Joyce Brothers~

> *It's not what you are that is holding you back. It's what you think you are not.*
> **~Anonymous~**

Most fears of rejection rest on the desire for approval from other people. Don't base your self-esteem on their opinions.
~Harvey Mackay~

Talk to yourself like you would to someone you love.
~Brene Brown~

Beauty begins the moment you decide to be yourself.
~CoCo Chanel~

Wanting to be someone else is a waste of the person you are.
~Marilyn Monroe~

You are perfect exactly as you are. With all your flaws and problems, there's no need to change anything. All you need to change is the thought that you aren't good enough.

~J. Cole~

Learning to love yourself will be the hardest thing you'll ever do in life.
~Unknown~

Self-love, self-respect and self-worth. There is a reason they all start with "self". You cannot find them in anyone else.

~Unknown~

Never forget that walking away from something unhealthy is BRAVE even if you stumble a little on your way out the door.
~Mandy Hale~

Look for something positive in each day, even if you have to look a little harder some days.
~Unknown~

> *Be more determined than your problems.*
> ~Billy Cox~

The Lord uses Ordinary People to Carry Out His Extraordinary plan.
~Unknown~

ABOUT THE AUTHOR

SIERRA DEAN is a St. Louis native, who believes heavily in empowering women. She is constantly uplifting women everywhere she goes, with her loving spirit. She is an advocate for Domestic Violence and volunteers at several non-profit organizations. Her humble attitude has her through all of life's challenges, which created her thick skin. Sierra's experiences and loving heart, has inspired others to do better and be better.

Made in the USA
Middletown, DE
13 July 2016